GW00724776

PLAYSETS CO

Isabeau

A play

Don Roberts

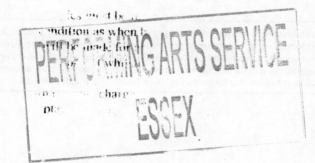

Samuel French—London
New York-Toronto-Hollywood

ISBN 0 573 12123 0

Please see page iv for further copyright information

CHARACTERS

Isabeau, a woman in her early twenties
Pascal, the café owner, a man in his late forties
Victor, a wine salesman in his mid-twenties
Yann, a lorry driver in his mid-to late twenties,
physically Victor's superior

The action takes place in a café in a Latin country

Time— this year or last year, in high summer

For Elizabeth, Sophy and Charlotte
and impressions of many byways
between Romorantin, Sisteron, Bronté and Ronda

Also by Don Roberts published by Samuel French Ltd

The Ragwoman of the Shambles
The Umbrella God
The Garden Room

ISABEAU

An empty café in a Latin country

Toward the rear is a small bar with coffee-making equipment and an assortment of cutlery lying in an orderly fashion on a couple of napkins. There are several small tables in the room, with all except one of the chairs upside-down on them. A blue windbreaker hangs on a hook by the door

When the CURTAIN *rises, the light is the soft light of an early morning; during the course of the play it grows gradually more intense*

Isabeau, a youngish woman, in a cheapish blouse and tatty jeans, sits awkwardly on a spindly chair by one of the tables, smoking and looking down at her bare feet, which she waggles from side to side. Her sandals lie half under her chair. A dish of coffee sits on the floor and a tatty rucksack lies nearby. On the table is an ashtray, a crumpled but recognizable packet of cigarettes and a clip of paper matches

The sound of a key is heard, then that of a door opening and closing

Isabeau looks up and appears calm as she waits

Pascal, a middle-aged man, enters. His white summer jacket is a little soiled and he wears a tie and cloth trousers that do not match the jacket. He sees Isabeau, stops instantly and speaks quietly but threateningly

Pascal Who are you?

Isabeau I've been here all night.

Pascal I thought I locked up properly.

Isabeau I heard you do it.

Pascal (*coming closer to Isabeau and looking hard at her*) I recognize you now: you're the grubby girl who came in late and begged to do washing up in exchange for a meal.

Isabeau You said I got all the pans clean.

Pascal I thought I saw you leave.

Isabeau I hid.

Pascal Where?

Isabeau Behind the aprons hanging in the kitchen.

Pascal Nowhere to go?

Isabeau There was the grandmother of a thunderstorm.

Pascal You might have been locked in all day. Mondays, I don't open until seven.

Isabeau seems to consider the implication of this, but keeps her thoughts to herself

Isabeau Will you send for the police?

Pascal I came in specially because a wine salesman rang unexpectedly saying could he see me this morning as a special favour. I haven't time to bother about the police, too much to do. I see you've made yourself coffee.

Isabeau stares at him, taking in his words

Isabeau Would you like coffee?

Pascal I won't refuse what's my own. Three spoons of sugar.

Isabeau I had a wash-down.

Pascal You needed it. (*He sniffs*) Look better for it.

Isabeau You won't find a trace of a mess, I cleaned up.

Pascal Are you hungry?

Isabeau Why are you being kind to me?

Pascal You seem in need of it.

Isabeau I haven't eaten.
Pascal You will find breakfast biscuits under the bar.

Isabeau stubs her cigarette out in the ash tray with some force, takes up her cup and goes to the bar, where she prepares the coffee. Pascal stares after Isabeau thoughtfully, then lifts the chairs off a nearby table and sits down on one of them. He pulls papers out of his pockets, unfolds them and spreads them on the table. He looks towards the bar. After a minute Isabeau returns with two coffees. She serves one to Pascal and keeps the other for herself, returning to her place

Isabeau The butter was in the fridge. I've put it out to soften.
Pascal How long have you been on the road?
Isabeau Almost lost count. (*She pauses to think*) Nearly four months.
Pascal Where do you come from?
Isabeau It stank.
Pascal How far away?
Isabeau Somewhere the other side of the mountains. A hundred miles. You wouldn't know. But I've wandered all over the place.
Pascal Why did you leave?
Isabeau There was no reason to stay.
Pascal (*stirring his coffee thoughtfully*) Are you on your own?
Isabeau Mostly. I go my own way.

Pascal sips his coffee and seems to be considering her answer

Pascal What work did you do back there?
Isabeau Women's work!
Pascal What's that?
Isabeau That's work the men won't do.
Pascal But you washed up for me?

Isabeau drains her coffee before answering

Isabeau Washing up's nothing.

Pascal You could feed yourself that way.

Isabeau I don't like kitchens, don't like to be a skivvy.

Pascal Do you want work?

Isabeau I do odd jobs to eat. I've kept myself and earned a bit to carry me over the days I don't work. That's when I travel. I couldn't beg.

Pascal The butter is probably soft by now. Eat while you can.

Isabeau Do you want anything?

Pascal (*draining his coffee*) Another coffee. There's enough for two.

Isabeau It's your coffee. (*She collects both cups*)

Pascal You're a conundrum.

Isabeau It's the way I am. (*She returns to the bar with the coffee cups*)

Pascal stares after Isabeau, then seems to look at his papers, moving them about, ticking with a pencil and making notes but constantly looking up as if anticipating Isabeau's return. He whistles to himself

Isabeau returns with a tray on which are two cups of coffee, a plate of breakfast biscuits, a knife, a saucer of jam, and butter. She puts the tray on her table, and then brings Pascal a coffee

Pascal If you worked here tonight, you could sleep in the storeroom. Serve the customers and clean up. Freshened up, you look acceptable and I'm often short-handed. Pay you, there'll be tips and you'll be fed.

Isabeau Can't stay. I want to go on. You wouldn't understand.

Pascal Many years ago I walked from place to place. About your age. I told myself I would always want to go on and on. But when I came to these parts, I stayed. (*He takes up his coffee and drinks it*)

Isabeau (*staring at him in disbelief*) Why did you stay?

Pascal I was tired and felt there wasn't any need to go any further.

Isabeau I'm not tired.

Pascal Pray you soon will be, then put down roots.

Isabeau (*violently*) I'm sick of roots, I want to be free.

Pascal And you're alone?

Isabeau From choice.

Pascal I'm alone. But not from choice.

Isabeau That's why you're kind to me!

Pascal You sound as if you hate kindness.

Isabeau Men always want something in return.

Pascal If you want to be rid of any obligation, help me check the stock.

Isabeau You'd better call the police.

Pascal There's no need. The door's unlocked if you want to go, there's nothing to stop you. You can go now.

Isabeau I'll finish my breakfast. Then go.

Pascal I gave it to you. I don't take back what I give.

Isabeau So you don't play God.

Pascal You forget I was on the road once and I'm grateful to God for kindnesses. Last year he took my wife.

Isabeau He doesn't exist, and if he did, he's never noticed me, never given me anything. And if he had, he would have taken it away. In the stinking place I come from, people always had God in their mouths.

Pascal contemplates her for a moment as if digesting her remark and disagreeing with it

Pascal So that is why you left.

Isabeau I told you, nothing to stay for.

Pascal But something drove you away? Did in my case, never regretted leaving. Never returned.

Isabeau Nothing happened, left of my own free will, and now I do everything of my own free will.

Pascal We all say that.

Isabeau Perhaps you don't mean it. You probably think you own this café, but really it owns you!(*Almost violently*) When I said "Of my own free will", I meant it. I'm going where I like, living how I like, taking what I like. I'm free.

Pascal (*smiling mysteriously*) Another coffee?

Isabeau looks for a moment as if she is going to refuse angrily, but she controls herself, subdued by his smile

Isabeau No, two's enough.

Pascal Something more to eat before you go. You've eaten very little.

Isabeau (*after a pause*) Another biscuit? (*Then, as if this is an afterthought*) Please.

Pascal rises, collects his cup and goes to the bar. He pours himself another coffee

Pascal An aperitif?

Isabeau No, I don't drink alone with a man.

Pascal pours out an aperitif for himself, picks up his coffee and a tin of biscuits and carries all three over to his seat. He sits and holds the biscuit tin out to Isabeau

Pascal Take as many as you want. Then, if you won't help with the stock, you'd better go. I've work to do.

Isabeau Because I wouldn't drink with you?

Pascal You can put it that way if you want to. But no, it's because you're against things, I've no patience with that. People like that go on walking the roads for ever.

There is the sound of a door opening and closing

Victor enters. He is a young man, dressed in a loose jacket and smart trousers with his shirt fastened but without a tie. He is carrying a case. He glimpses Isabeau and then looks sharply at her

(*Rising and shaking Victor by the hand*) Ah! One thing I can depend on with you, Victor. Always on time with your calls, never keep me waiting.

Victor I know it's the way you do business. I'm sorry I had to fix up to meet you without proper warning. As I told you, I'm making calls earlier in the month because we've brought out a new list. There's been a lot of changes since the son came into the business. Better choice. More adventurous wines. Revised prices. New terms. The son's more or less running things now. Itineraries have been changed, complete overhaul! The old man only comes in a couple of mornings a week these days.

Pascal So I've heard. Not the way to do things in my opinion. The old man's either in the trade or out of it. Customers never know where they are when things are like that. Would you like a coffee? Or something else, Victor?

Victor A coffee, I'll get it myself. Give you a chance to look over the list.

Pascal She can get it and get me another one. Come on, young lady, help pay for your night in the dry. Then you can give the chairs a bit of a dust, you'll find everything behind the bar.

Isabeau glares but goes over to the coffee machine. Victor takes a chair off a table, takes a list out of the case and gives it to Pascal. Victor sits and watches Isabeau drawing two coffees. He smiles slightly as he scrutinizes her. Pascal runs a pencil expertly over the wine list

Victor (*to Isabeau*) Hullo! You're a new face. Working for Mr Pascal?

Pascal She washed up last night, then dossed down here out of the storm.

Isabeau I hid. He found me this morning and stood me breakfast.

Victor You going to be working here?

Isabeau What he wants, but it's not on. I'm on the road, going here and there as the mood takes me. A job here for a day or two, a job there. Whatever catches my eye.

Isabeau brings two cups of coffee to the men and then walks away, with every show of indifference

Pascal Half of your list is new. There are things here that interest me, but the prices are higher than I pay.

Victor For an old customer of the firm, there will be discounts and we're giving longer to pay. We're offering a wider selection of better wines. And there's a section of fine wines.

Pascal I don't want fine wines. Haven't found any I don't know like the back of my hand.

Victor Your café is thriving. With finer wines...

Pascal Reliable prices are what my customers expect. Reliable wines at fair prices. And what you list as your fine wines, aren't! I know what's what. Have to have more than the name of the proprietor and a year on a fancy label. Victor, four or five times a year I drink fine wines myself and enjoy them. But I wouldn't serve them. I serve good country food and they wouldn't suit. You should know me and the trade in my café better than to try me with fine wines. But you've your job to do, I know that. You can tell your young master from me that no self-respecting café owner is going to buy his so-called fine wines. Know too much.

Victor signals that he accepts Pascal's point by a deprecating movement of the hands, as if in the hope of stopping his flow

Are you listening to me or eyeing that girl?

Victor I'm listening. What I'm paid to do.

Pascal Suppose you might as well eye her while you can. Your only chance, she won't stay. Girls move on to the bigger towns just as soon as they start being useful. You never hear of them again.

Victor I can't help you with getting girls! (*He turns directly to*

Isabeau) This little town's prosperous.

Pascal Tips are good. Especially market days.

Victor You ought to stay here, young lady.

Isabeau I've no wish to stay. Looks the sort of place that's empty in the winter.

Victor Pascal's the greatest café owner in the town. And for miles around, if it comes to that. He'll teach you the trade.

Isabeau I'll go soon. But first I'll clear up. (*She collects the dirty cups and glasses and takes them to the bar, where she washes them during the following dialogue*)

Pascal This list is for me to mark, isn't it? All over the place. Why did you have to muck it up? I'll check my stock now. Then tie up the order and you can be on your way. You're still not selling to anyone else in the neighbourhood?

Victor We understand that. There's no-one else here.

Pascal Make sure it stays that way, Victor.

Pascal rises, and with his own papers and the list in his hand, exits

Victor (*calling out*) They know that, I've made it clear.

Pascal gives a smothered grunt of approval off stage

Victor slowly turns to look at Isabeau, straightening a little wad of papers as he does so. He takes time to make sure Pascal is out of hearing

Didn't expect to find you here.

Isabeau I saw you knew me again.

Victor You didn't let on.

Isabeau Why should I?

Victor A bit off your patch? (*He turns his chair towards Isabeau*)

Isabeau No such place as my patch. I go where I please.

Victor When I gave you lifts, you went where I wanted.

Isabeau Suited me...

Victor How did you get here?

Isabeau A couple of long-distance lorry drivers picked me up.

Victor You didn't waste much time finding a bloke to give you a lift.

Isabeau I spoke to him when he was filling up. We didn't stop on the way. Just dropped me off here and went on.

Victor I must have been specially favoured.

Isabeau Not now you aren't! Not since you short-changed me the second time.

Victor Didn't realize it was business. I thought it was for the fun of the thing. And the price of a slap-up meal and that hop.

Isabeau I kept my side of the agreement.

Victor rises and walks almost tantalisingly towards Isabeau

Are you going to offer me a cigarette?

Victor That was one of my cigarettes you've just finished! You stole them.

Isabeau You saw. Didn't seem to mind, too intent on ... (*She laughs mockingly*)

Victor produces a packet of cigarettes and offers one to Isabeau. She takes one. Victor takes a cigarette himself and lights them both with his lighter

Victor Take another.

Isabeau Stick to this brand and we might meet again.

Victor You're pretty sure of yourself. What makes you think I want to?

Isabeau I don't think, I know.

Victor I can reckon that a couple of times a week, there's a girl hitching a lift. I'm kind, I give lifts — not so many drivers do these days — and girls fall for my charm, take a fancy to me. I'm a good-looking enough guy. You and I took a fancy to one another, natural! You're not the first, won't be the last. That's the way life is. Anyway you're not that special that I should stick with that brand of cigarette.

Isabeau I'm special. Last week when I saw you in the car park at the petrol station I fancied you. You'd caught my eye earlier, when you arrived. I'd never had a lift in a car like yours, it looked fast and is a beautiful orange. I followed you, got myself a cup of coffee and took a second look at you. Then I went outside and waited, asked for a lift, knowing you couldn't refuse. You like showing off, all salesmen are the same. (*She moves away from Victor and fetches a duster, brush and small dustpan from behind the bar. She starts cleaning chairs and setting them down on the floor during the following dialogue, occasionally picking up the odd piece of rubbish from the floor*)

Victor Rubbish! I'm not an easy catch. You were on your uppers, desperate for a free meal and pocket money.

Isabeau You'd caught my eye, I lay in wait and you were mine.

Victor Dozens of girls want lifts. You're just one among hundreds.

Isabeau Yesterday you drove by me like fury. Then suddenly you screeched to a halt, and backed. Backing fast. I recognized the car, knew it was you. I hadn't even hitched a lift. You begged me to get in. And when I walked on, you followed me. I went on walking, you went on begging. So I took pity on you. I thought I might as well prove I'm special. But I didn't think you'd short-change me. Half what we agreed.

Victor I didn't short-change you, you were greedy and you aren't that special. (*He closes in on Isabeau during the following*)

Isabeau I kept my side of the bargain, expect you to keep yours now you've turned up here. I thought you were supposed to be a long way away. Or was that another of your stories?

Victor Don't think I followed you; I didn't.

Isabeau I'm thinking about it.

Victor You're not anything to boast about, no better than any of the other girls who hitch lifts. Not what I'd call special.

Isabeau You know you're a bad liar.

Victor I said you're not that special.

Isabeau Not what you said yesterday. Not the way you begged me. I saw the look in your eyes. I could make you follow me, make you wait for me, make you do as I want. I could make you do all those things if I wanted to.(*She flaps her duster at him and jumps out of his range*)

Victor If I picked you up it's because I took pity on you. Get that clear, girlie, I ain't —

Isabeau (*cutting him short*) If I left here and didn't tell you which way I was going, north or south, you'd drive up and down trying to find me. I saw the lost look in your face when we parted. I saw hunger when you came in here, though you tried to hide it. Yesterday, you begged me to stay with you, and I said "No, I don't stay with anyone". Understand! I do everything of my own free will.

Victor does not immediately answer: when he does his manner has changed. He tries to touch Isabeau but she evades him

Victor I'll wait at the top end of the village. Tag along for a few days. Please. Nice hotels. See you get a lift the way you want to go. Give you a good time. Please.

Isabeau I'll go as the mood takes me. Think of me as a bird. I do.

There is the sound of Pascal returning. Victor returns to his place and sits down quickly

Victor I'd stay here if I were you. Food's good, tips are good. He's straight and there's lots that aren't. I know, I have to deal with them. Right bastards, some of them.

Pascal enters with the list, now marked up, in his hand

Pascal I've been through your list and marked it. You've got a good order; you know I don't live hand-to-mouth. But before I hand it over, something to get straight, Victor: your arrangements and charges for delivery are still the same?

Victor For old customers like you, Pascal, there's no charge.

Pascal I'd like that in writing. Items marked with a red cross, I want within three weeks. The balance — that's the items marked with a black cross — I want in six weeks. And I've ordered half-dozens of five of your new wines. If I don't like them, I want credit. I've put circles around them. Half a dozen first, then if I like them, four dozen when I say so. See! (*He holds out the list to Victor*)

Victor crosses the room to read the list. Pascal waits calmly, keeping hold of the list while Victor scans it

Victor Looks in order to me. I'll deal with it.

Pascal See you do! I want the full quantity price for the new wines I've ordered half dozens of, otherwise you needn't bother. I'll try them but not at my risk.

Victor I'll have to ask the new boss that.

Pascal You ask him. But I tell you that either I get the discount or you needn't deliver any of them at all. There's other merchants about will give me the same deal. Or better. The Co-operative certainly will. I've been in this business longer than your new boss has had long trousers. He can start learning. I'm not.

Victor I understand. (*He changes the subject*) Been telling this young lady she should stay.

Pascal That's up to her.

Victor Dry weather's coming to an end. I told her that.

Pascal She's got a month.

Isabeau I'm going south. Stays warmer longer and the rains don't come till later.

Victor If you want to start south today, I'm going that way. Could take you a matter of forty miles; it's a start.

Isabeau Haven't decided when I'm going. If I like the look of a place, I take a couple of days off, then move on. What I saw last night looked good.

Victor You've got half an hour to decide. My car's across the
square.

Isabeau I don't make my mind up that fast. And if I want a
lift south, there's always lorry drivers glad of a bit of
company.

Pascal Why don't you take your couple of days off? And,
tonight, come here around six and help serve, or around ten
and wash up. Patrons like to see a new face. Either way, I'll
pay, give you a meal and there's a camp bed in the
storeroom. It'll be damp out of doors, rain doesn't go that
quick.

Isabeau If I stayed, could I wash a few of my things out?

Pascal There's a yard out the back where they'll dry. Catches
the sun.

Isabeau I'll think about it.

Pascal I'm sure you will. Can't make you out. Do you just say
things to put people off?

Isabeau Then don't try.

Pascal You're not on the run?

Isabeau No. Put me down as ordinary.

Pascal Ordinary sounds as if men would pass by and not
notice you. You're wrong there. Victor's noticed you, right,
lad?

Victor She catches the eye, you're right there! (*He laughs*)

Pascal Here's your list, don't know why you have to muddle
everything up! It doesn't help the customers to change
things.

Victor (*glancing over the list*) There's a sheet missing. Didn't
you want any spirits and aperitifs?

Pascal Damn! I know where I've left it. Give me a minute.

Pascal rises and goes out

Victor watches Pascal go, then moves to Isabeau

Victor Please! I'm going any minute now.

Isabeau You're a fool. Please! (*She takes a few mincing steps in mockery of him, but he doesn't respond*) Please! Please what?

Victor Come with me! Don't stay here. He'll work you to death.

Isabeau I haven't made my mind up. And nobody works me to death. I'll do as I please. I thought you said I wasn't that special. But now you're saying please. (*Mockingly*) Please!

Victor Give you a good time.

Isabeau A good time?

Victor You know — a good time!

Isabeau Like the others who came and went.

Victor Please Isabeau!

Isabeau (*mocking his tone*) Please Isabeau!

Victor moves towards Isabeau as if to touch or embrace her

Stay there! A step nearer and you can give up hope.

He stands rooted, glaring at her. She seems to hold him fixed as a snake does a rabbit, and flicks her duster repeatedly at him as if it is the tongue of a snake

Sit down and I might think about it. (*She imitates him*) Please!

Victor You're playing with me! I have the feeling ... I know there's somebody you're hanging around for.

Isabeau There's nobody I'd hang around for.

Victor You didn't come straight here. I followed the lorry. It stopped in the village car park for half an hour before you got out and it went on.

Isabeau He came from my village.

Victor Don't believe you.

Isabeau That's up to you.

Victor I followed you here, had to see you again, I had to know where you'd gone. I waited outside for you to come out. And when you didn't come, I thought Pascal had given

    you a job; I'd seen you talking to him. Then it threatened a
    storm. So I telephoned him — wasn't due till next week.

Isabeau So I am special.

Victor I'm a sucker. I treated you to meals, stuffed notes in
    your hands; you steal my cigarettes, you mock me and I
    follow you.

Isabeau Shall I tell him you followed me?

Victor No! I don't know how he would react.

Isabeau He'd laugh. He might send you away without an
    order.

Victor Don't tell him then. (*He laughs uneasily*) Pascal can be
    jealous!

Isabeau Perhaps I'll stay here. He's on his own.

Victor No! Isabeau, please come with me. You have to or I'll
    go crazy.

Isabeau Does he pay well? Better than you?

Pascal is heard returning.

Victor (*controlling himself*) Ask him yourself, he's fair, I
    know that. But you have to work hard, and work the way he
    says. But don't stay; come with me; that would be better for
    both of us, give you a good time. Promise! I'll ——

Pascal is heard, coming very close

    It's not a bad village, very busy on market days; people are
    prosperous, give-ish.

Pascal enters with the list

Pascal I found the sheet. Forgotten to mark it, but now I have.
    You're getting a good order today. But if I don't get good
    terms, it'll be your last.

Victor I'll make sure you get the best terms. I want to be able
    to come back here.

Pascal We'll have a cognac to seal the bargain. And you, young lady! And think about staying. You have to work hard, and work the way I say. But I'm fair. And there's a comfortable bed in the dry.

Victor and Isabeau react; it is obvious that Pascal has overheard at least part of their conversation

Girls who work for me get a good training. Trouble is, they leave me and go on to what they think are better things in the big towns. And I get left on my own and have to start again.*(He begins to dispense cognac into three glasses)*

Victor I told her you were fair — best café owner around about.

Isabeau Whether I stay or go is nothing to do with you. I decide things for myself. No man tells me what to do. In five minute's time, I'll walk out of here and go wherever the mood takes me, up one street, down another, look in the river from the bridge, just as the mood takes me. If I return tonight, it will be because I like the look of this place for a few days — no more. If I stay it will be because of my own free will, not your words, nor his.

Pascal Of your own free will then! But at six tonight or ten, you'll be welcome to work here. There'll be plenty of work, I promise you, hard work. Same terms as last night, some money in your pocket and as much food as you can eat. And a bed for the night.

There is the sound of a window being tapped violently to attract attention

Pascal hesitates for a moment, then gives a cognac each to Victor and Isabeau. He leaves the bottle of cognac on the counter or on a table top

Pascal Can't he read "Closed". There's always someone who does this if I come in on Monday!

Pascal hurries out

Victor and Isabeau taste their cognac, watching one another

The knocking is repeated, louder and more forcibly

Pascal (*off*) I'm shut! Open at seven.
Yann (*off*) You've got a girl here!

Isabeau stiffens and seems apprehensive for a moment. Victor, observing her, seems to listen intently

There is the sound of a door being rattled

Pascal (*off*) No need to break the door down.

There is the sound of the door being opened

Yann (*off*) You've got a girl in here. Isabeau! Isabeau!

> *Yann, a youngish, burly man in sharp physical contrast to Victor, erupts into the room. He is wearing blue bib overalls with an unbuttoned windbreaker over them. Pascal follows him in*

(*To Isabeau*) So you are here! I've come to take you home. No life for a woman the way you're living, Isabeau! Going from place to place, not settled.
Isabeau I decide what's my life. And I'm staying here, settled. I'm taking his job. Go away, Yann.

Pascal goes to the bar and pours himself a cognac. He listens intently to the following

Yann You're to come back with me.
Isabeau No.
Yann To where you belong.

Isabeau I've left for good.

Yann You haven't. You can never leave for good. It's inside you.

Isabeau Nothing's inside me. And nobody tells me what to do. I've left for good. I hate the thought of the place, the sight of it, the smell of it, the stinking stillness of summer, the bitter wind in autumn, the snow glare in winter. I hate everything about it. I want to forget its name and its people. (*She strikes her heart*) And I hate in here and you know that can't be changed.

Yann stares at her like a cat and his body bends as though about to pounce

Yann Why hate me?

Isabeau Don't try to force me.

Yann I was kind to you.

Isabeau hesitates for a moment before replying

Isabeau You tried to be kind. I don't hate you. But that's no reason for going back. I'm free of the place now; it's a wonderful feeling and I'm not giving it up.

Yann You've been wandering from place to place, living hand to mouth, sleeping God knows where. You said so. You can't call that free. It's got no future.

Isabeau I've changed, can't you see I've changed?

Yann I recognized you.

Isabeau Please, leave me alone, Yann. You'll do no good.

Victor You heard what he said. Leave her alone!

Yann stares at Victor threateningly for a moment; his next words have no trace of violent feelings, however

Yann Who are you?

Victor A friend! She'll tell you that.

Yann Friend? You gave her a lift, that's all. I recognize you.

Saw you drop her off somewhere. She doesn't need your sort for friends, she needs her own people.

Victor Says she hates them, you heard her!

Yann You know nothing. Down your drink and go. I have things to settle.

Pascal comes forward rapidly, signalling with his hands to quieten things. Victor looks intimidated

Pascal No more of this. It's my café and I decide things here. So sit down, my young friend, join us, let me pour you a cognac. Then perhaps we can talk. And let the girl decide things for herself. I'm short-staffed.

Yann I don't want your cognac. Whatever you offer me, I'll refuse. I haven't any time to waste.

Pascal Listen to me, please. This is my place and I don't like unpleasantness. My hospitality is usually accepted.

Yann I don't listen to strangers. I know what has to be done. You can listen if you want. Isabeau has been missing for months. Her family has been searching. Wherever I've driven I've looked out for her, asked about her. Sometimes I've heard about her or a girl like her. Seen the way they live. Other men might have given up, but not me. I went on looking. Then last night, without warning, I found her by a petrol station on the main road. She promised to be here in this village today when I'd delivered my load. I spent the last half an hour looking for her round the square, wondering if she'd keep her word. Then I saw her shadow on your window, so I came at once.

Isabeau I promised to talk to you because you'd been kind to me. I never promised to go back.

Yann Come outside. I don't want to talk in front of strangers.

Isabeau We talk here. I don't care if they hear or not. They're only men like you.

Yann This is not right. What I have to say is for you and no-one else.

Isabeau It's the way I want things. And be quick. This is where I work, and there's work to be done soon. And if you can't be quick, go!

Yann You're playing some kind of trick on me, I feel it.

Isabeau I never bother with tricks. Never been my way and I haven't changed.

Yann Finish your drink. Then we'll go. I want you to come back. Today.

Isabeau So you're the messenger. The warder. The man the village sent looking for me.

Yann My lorry is my work, you know it takes me all over the country. I kept looking and I kept asking. I found you by chance and I found you for myself. But your brothers and your grandfather will be happy to see you home.

Isabeau I was good with the cows,wasn't I! Good at milking. Good at going halfway up the mountain to move the cattle to the summer pastures, as good as any lad in the village, and cheaper, I didn't have to be paid or taken drinking. And I can't inherit a share because I'm a woman and my mother couldn't remember who she lay with at the horse fair. That's why my grandfather and my half-brothers will be content to have me back: to work myself to the bone.

Yann They've missed you; they love you.

Isabeau When the news came that I had passed my school exams with honours, they locked me in the barn for a week in case I ran away, and brought me bread and an apple twice a day when they could find the time. The day they let me out, they beat me to "Get rid of the learning " and made me clean the pigsties. That's how much they loved me.

Yann They're sorry for that, they told me so. They haven't told the village you ran away; they think you're over the mountains with the Good Sisters of Charity for six months. You'll be welcomed with open arms.

Isabeau They'll welcome me with a beating. Then set me cleaning the pigsties.

Yann I won't let them, Isabeau.

Isabeau You're a simple, kind soul, Yann. You'll believe them and you won't know they've beaten me till it's too late.

And you won't interfere, the men always beat the women in our village, it's what they've been doing all their lives and what their grandfathers and *their* grandfathers did. Nobody will raise a hand to stop it. Not even the priest. But I'm not going back to be beaten. Yann, you go on your way without me.

Yann I'm not going back alone. They've agreed that if I bring you back, I marry you.

Victor seems about to intervene, but is cautioned by a gesture from Pascal, who is listening intently like a man who is reliving an experience. Isabeau does not immediately answer. Victor moves uneasily in his seat, as if he feels increasingly threatened

Isabeau Whatever they promised, I'm not coming back.

Yann I love you. It's always been that way.

Isabeau I knew you wanted me when I ran away. It was another reason for going. I looked at the other girls and told myself that I wasn't going to be like them, mother to a household of children, unpaid hand in the fields, up early every day with the cows, while the man was away in the outside world doing as he pleased — you, away with your big truck delivering God knows where and keeping every penny. Now will you go away, Yann. I hate the village and its ways. It's why I worked at school — to escape.

Yann (*his manner softening*) I don't understand you. I hate being away from the village, always long to be home. You have to come back with me.

Isabeau You don't understand. Men are all the same!

Victor (*seeing his chance*) I understand. Isabeau's told you she won't go back with you. She's escaped. As far as she's concerned, I've as much right to her as you have. Or anybody else. And she's staying that way.

There is a pause. Pascal looks uneasy, as if afraid that Yann will become violent

Yann How long have you known her?

Victor A day or two. But it's long enough.

Yann That's nothing. You have nothing to do with us, stranger. You're not from our village. I've known her all my life. She's coming back with me and we're going to be married.

Isabeau No-one owns me. I'm not marrying anyone.

Yann It's what all young girls say. They change when they've a baby at the breast. You've been silly long enough.(*He puts out his hands as if to take Isabeau*)

Pascal Wait! This is not your village, young man! It's my café. The world has left your village behind. You drive all over the country with your lorry; you must see that. And she wants to work for me.

Yann I drive for money. I go home at least once a week, and give thanks I come from my village. Everything there has its place; life is simple and good. There I breathe.

Isabeau You're not a fool,Yann. You don't mean to be cruel. Blind is what you are. If you're a man, life in the village is simple and good. But women suffocate there; the only life is escape.

Yann When you're back, you'll see things differently.

Isabeau I'd rather die.

Yann You always were a proud one. I'll boast of that in the years to come.

Victor You won't boast about her. She's not coming with you.

Isabeau Enough! I speak for myself. I'm free, free to do as I like. Free to go, free to stay. I will not be suffocated by men, any of you. I won't stay with anyone.

Yann and Victor are momentarily silenced

Pascal Let the girl have some days to herself, some days to think. There's always work for her here, and a place to sleep. I think you gentlemen should leave and go about your business elsewhere. She'll make her own way when she decides to go.

Yann I'm not leaving without Isabeau. She's marrying me, her family agreed. And I love her.

Isabeau Go away, Yann, forget me. There are girls in the village willing to give you sons and sew you shirts.

Yann You're promised to me. The village knows, believes you're with the Sisters till I claim you. (*He pauses*) I can't return without you, having found you. We'll marry the Sunday after we return and all the village will dance at our wedding.

Isabeau I'll not marry you.

Yann You will marry me; it's agreed. I can't return to our village without you.

Isabeau I'll not stand up in church wearing white. Nor hide the truth from you. When I've wanted a man, I've taken a young one from the crowd. I don't belong to anyone now. I claim my own!

Yann But you were promised to me, promised ...

Isabeau I made no promise. I take.

Yann Take!

Isabeau Now you're listening. Take a young man whenever I fancy.

Yann Take ...! Where ...?

Isabeau You have to search the crowd. That's where my young men are: scattered! (*She laughs defiantly*) Yann, forget me. You've got years of life behind and ahead of you. Now I'm claiming my own.

Yann Claiming your own?(*He seems to be thinking slowly, resisting the thoughts*) How many men, Isabeau, tell me how many men? You're promised to me, don't you understand? I can't go back to the village without you, I can't go back .... Don't believe you, it's a trick .... Show me a single man ...!

Isabeau (*looking provocatively at Yann and pointing to Victor*) Him for one.

Yann (*in disbelief*) Him?

Isabeau You asked me. Him! There he is.

Yann (*moving towards Victor; disbelievingly*) That!

Victor (*panicking*) Can't you understand! Isabeau doesn't want you, Isabeau doesn't want me! She's not going to belong to either of us. She just takes! Then throws away!

Yann You made love to her. She's promised to me! The village knows.

Yann lets out a terrible cry like an animal and jumps on Victor, who manages to slide partly out of his grasp, though he is still held

Pascal Stop! Stop!

Yann (*beginning to force Victor's head back*) I'll break your neck!

Victor frees one of his hands

Isabeau Yann, you're obsessed. Let him go! Listen to me! I'll never belong to either of you! Never! Not to anybody! Not made that way! Stop fighting. (*She appeals to Pascal*) Stop them! Can't you stop them? Help me.

Pascal moves as if to intervene. Yann's fury, and his grip on Victor, increases. They slither backwards in their struggle. Victor breaks free, but seems unable to run away, only to back away with his eyes fixed on Yann. Yann lets the gap between them grow, so that when it is large enough he will pounce. Victor, terrified, moves slowly backwards between the tables. His hand comes in contact with the bar and then with the pile of cutlery on it. The fingers of his right hand find the handle of a carving knife and in panic he sweeps the knife round, holding it in front of him

Victor Leave me alone. I've got a knife! Back off or I'll use it.

Pascal Stop it. Both of you!

Yann, enraged, crouches and thrusts himself forward. Pascal tries to hold Yann but is swept aside; he then cautiously approaches the combatants, unable to intervene. Yann rushes at Victor and grabs him; in doing so, he drives himself on to the knife in Victor's hand. Yann lets out an almost silent cry and slowly releases his grip on Victor, his face assuming a look of surprise. He looks down and feels with his hand until he finds the knife sticking out of him. He slides to the floor, his expression one of disbelief. He groans, kicks for a moment, and then is still. Victor is rooted to the spot as if horror-stricken and unable to believe what he has done

Pascal goes quickly to the dead man, grasps his face and looks into his eyes

Isabeau (*moving fearfully towards the body*) Yann ...! Oh no ...!
Victor Have I ...?

Pascal slips his hand into Yann's shirt. He looks up and nods significantly to Victor

Pascal Done for ...
Victor Never meant to ... Not possible ... So quick!
Pascal It is, sometimes. Running on a knife, goes in deep.
Isabeau Yann! Oh, no! (*She appeals to Pascal and holds out a hand in his direction*) Help us, help us! Please!
Victor So quick.... What have I done? (*He looks hopelessly at his right hand, then at Isabeau*) Trying to save myself .... I didn't mean to, Isabeau .... (*His voice chokes on the words*) Pascal, are you going to send for the police...? Pascal, I didn't mean to ....

Pascal searches in Yann's pockets and in the second one he comes to he finds the keys to Yann's lorry. He rises and forces the keys into Victor's hand

Pascal Listen carefully! Find his lorry — you know what it looks like — bring it round to my yard at the back. Don't run, take it easy, so nobody notices. I'll show you where to dump it and this poor fellow's body. We have to hope nobody knows he came here searching. Go slowly. Slowly, be ordinary. (*He turns Victor towards the door and more or less pushes him towards it*)

Isabeau begins to cry silently, as if the tears come from exhaustion

(*To Victor*) Stop! Not in that jacket. Take it off. There's a windbreaker by the door. Somebody left it here. Put it on as you go out. Look more like him.

Victor seems unable to move. Pascal propels Victor towards the windbreaker and helps him on with it

(*To Isabeau*) And you, child, go across the square and wait under the plane trees. You'll easily find a driver to take you south, keep going till you reach the sea, get a job, new clothes, then move on again and change your job, cut your hair differently. Forget you were ever here and heaven help you.

Victor exits slowly

Isabeau retreats slowly from Yann's body, her eyes fixed on him

Isabeau I can't go. (*She stops*) He was kind to me. It's true.
Pascal (*his voice rising to a shout during this speech*) Go! This is men's work. I'll see to it. You go! And do as I say. Do it quickly. And never remember you were ever in these parts. Now go! This is men's work!

Pascal propels Isabeau towards the door

They exit

The café is bathed in the brilliant light of the early morning sun as ——

- *the* CURTAIN *falls*

FURNITURE AND PROPERTY LIST

On stage: Bar *On it or in it*: bottles of wine, aperitifs, spirits etc,
including cognac, glasses, cups, saucers, plates, nap-
kins, cutlery (including carving-knife), coffee-making
equipment, tray, saucer of jam, butter in butter - dish, tin
of biscuits. *Behind it* : duster, brush, small dust pan
Several small tables. *On them* : chairs, upside-down
Table *On it* : ashtray, crumpled packet of cigarettes, clip
of paper matches. *On floor beside it:* chair
Dish of coffee
Rucksack
Sandals
On a hook near the door: blue windbreaker

Off stage :   Case containing list (**Victor**)
Second sheet of paper (**Pascal**)

Personal: **Pascal** : pencil, papers
Yann : keys

LIGHTING PLOT

Practical fittings required: nil
Interior. The same scene throughout

To open : Soft early morning light becoming progressively brighter
throughout play

No cues

EFFECTS PLOT

No cues